STARTERS
PEOPLE

D1826146

Geronimo

Macdonald Educational

This city is in America.
It is called Tucson.
Many people live and work in Tucson.

Many years ago the land
looked like this.
Only Apache Indians lived there.
Geronimo was one of their leaders.

Apache Indians lived in tribes.
They did not have tipis.
Instead, they built houses called wickiups.

The Apaches grew crops to eat.
The women planted the seeds.
The children helped at harvest-time.

The Apaches also hunted for food.
Sometimes they stole cattle
from other tribes.

The Apaches were good at hunting.
They rode for many miles
when they hunted.

When Geronimo was young, the Apaches
had the land to themselves.
Then white settlers began to come.

8

The white settlers wanted
to live on Apache land.
But the Apaches wanted
to keep it for themselves.

The settlers fought the Apaches
and took their land.

10

This made Geronimo very angry.
He talked to the leaders of other tribes.
They agreed to help him.

The Apache tribes tried
to get their land back.
They fought the white settlers.
The Apaches often won.

Then the settlers asked
the army to help.
They thought the army
could help them beat the Apaches.

The army had big guns and many soldiers.
Geronimo led the Apaches against the army.

The Apaches were good at fighting.
They were quick and clever.
They often beat the soldiers.

Fort Apache

So the army built forts.
It was easier to fight the Apaches
from the forts.

16

Fort Bowie

Now the army was able to win more battles.
They took much more Apache land.

17

Some Apaches surrendered to the army.
The soldiers wanted to capture Geronimo.
So he led his people to safety in Mexico.

The army wanted the fighting to stop.
They agreed to give the Apaches some land.
Geronimo came back to talk
to the army leaders.

But the army leaders would not
give the Apaches their homelands.
The Apaches were given land far away.

The Apaches did not like the new land.
They were not allowed to hunt.
They had to obey the army.

Geronimo started fighting again.
At last, the army agreed
to give the Apaches better land.

So the Apaches moved to the new land.
Geronimo and his tribe were tired.
They could not fight any more.

So after many years Geronimo settled down.
He and his family lived peacefully.
Geronimo was the last great Apache leader.

Today there are still Apaches in America.
Some of them breed pigs and cattle.

needle

elastic thread

dried melon seeds
or pumpkin seeds
or beads

String some seeds or beads together
for an Apache head-band.
You could also wear it as a necklace.

Index

Apache
Indian
(page 3)

cattle
(page 6)

tipi
(page 4)

guns
(page 14)

wickiup
(page 4)

soldier
(page 14)

crops
(page 5)

fort
(page 16)

Some facts about Geronimo and the Apaches

Geronimo was born in a place called
Nodoyohn Cañon in June 1829.
He grew up in the country
near the Gila River in Arizona.
He had three brothers and four sisters.

Geronimo belonged to the Chiricahua tribe.
There were three other main Apache tribes.
They were called the Mescalero tribe,
the Lipan tribe and the Jicarilla tribe.

Geronimo was not a chief. He was a war leader.
There were several famous Chiricahua chiefs.
Victoria was Chief of the Hot Springs Apaches.
Cochise and his son, Naiche, were Chiefs
of the Chokonen Apaches.
Whoa was Chief of the Nedni Apaches.
Mangas Coloradas was Chief of Geronimo's group.
This group was called the Bedonkohe Apaches.

All these chiefs fought together to get
their land back. They fought for 26 years.